# YOUR KNOWLEDGE HAS VALUE

- We will publish your bachelor's and
  master's thesis, essays and papers

- Your own eBook and book -
  sold worldwide in all relevant shops

- Earn money with each sale

Upload your text at www.GRIN.com
and publish for free

**Bibliographic information published by the German National Library:**

The German National Library lists this publication in the National Bibliography; detailed bibliographic data are available on the Internet at http://dnb.dnb.de .

This book is copyright material and must not be copied, reproduced, transferred, distributed, leased, licensed or publicly performed or used in any way except as specifically permitted in writing by the publishers, as allowed under the terms and conditions under which it was purchased or as strictly permitted by applicable copyright law. Any unauthorized distribution or use of this text may be a direct infringement of the author s and publisher s rights and those responsible may be liable in law accordingly.

**Imprint:**

Copyright © 2016 GRIN Verlag, Open Publishing GmbH
Print and binding: Books on Demand GmbH, Norderstedt Germany
ISBN: 9783656988533

**This book at GRIN:**

http://www.grin.com/en/e-book/335860/latin-american-revolutionary-augusto-cal-deron-sandino-an-analysis-of-his

Michael Gorman

# Latin American Revolutionary Augusto Calderón Sandino. An Analysis of His Credibility as a Revolutionary

GRIN Publishing

**GRIN - Your knowledge has value**

Since its foundation in 1998, GRIN has specialized in publishing academic texts by students, college teachers and other academics as e-book and printed book. The website www.grin.com is an ideal platform for presenting term papers, final papers, scientific essays, dissertations and specialist books.

**Visit us on the internet:**

http://www.grin.com/

http://www.facebook.com/grincom

http://www.twitter.com/grin_com

Latin American Revolutionary, Augusto Calderón Sandino

Michael Gorman

Jan 24, 2012

Latin American History 341

Thesis Proposal

In the late 1920s and early 1930s, Nicaragua, like many Latin American countries, was subject to corruption from within, and outside interference from foreign powers. President Adolfo Diaz of Nicaragua was corrupt and power hungry. Before coming to power, he worked as a secretary for the American owned and operated La Luz y Los Angeles Mining Company.

This company was chartered in Delaware and owned the large gold mines around Siuna in eastern Nicaragua. Through his employment, he helped channel funds to the revolt against the previous, liberal, President José Santos Zelaya, who had angered the United States by negotiating and proposing the construction of a Nicaragua Canal. Díaz with with Germany and Japan, instead of them. After becoming president, Díaz was forced to rely on the United States Marines to put down a Liberal revolt, which resulted in a deployment of Marines remaining in Nicaragua for over a decade. Later, in 1914, Diaz signed the Bryan-Chamorro Treaty, which granted the United States exclusive rights to build an inter-oceanic canal across Nicaragua.[1],[2] After leaving the presidency, he later returned in 1926, after a coup by General Emiliano Chamorro. His corruption and bid to remain in office triggered further revolts, causing him to call on the United States for support, and thus inciting further unrest and leading to the rise of Augusto Calderón Sandino, who waged a guerrilla war against Diaz and the United States Marines.[3]

The United States, under the guise of upholding the Monroe Doctrine, which provided the United States with the "right to protect and defend" countries within the American continents, engaged in a series of conflicts called the Banana Wars from about 1898-1934.[4] The United States' interventions in, and occupation of, Nicaragua, from 1912-1933, were part of

---

[1] Lau Gutiérrez, William. *Proceso de la intervención norteamericana en Nicaragua (1909 – 1913)*. Encuentro: Revista Académica de la Universidad Centroamericana, 1989.

[2] Bailey, Thomas, A. "Interest in a Nicaragua Canal, 1903-1931." *The Hispanic American Historical Review*. Vol. 16, No. 1 (Feb., 1936), pg. 2-28.

[3] Wünderich, Volker. *Sandino: Una biografía política*, Nicaragua: Editorial Nueva Nicaragua,1995.

[4] Langley, Lester D. *The Banana Wars: United States Intervention in the Caribbean, 1898–1934*. Kentucky: University Press of Kentucky, 1983.

these Banana Wars.[5] Despite the "official" intention being for the United States to maintain order and protect those who could not defend themselves, at this time, the United States military intervention in Nicaragua was designed to protect American business interests in the region, and stop any other nation except the United States from building a Nicaraguan Canal.[6],[7] This eventually caused Nicaragua to assume a quasi-protectorate status under the 1916 Bryan–Chamorro Treaty.[8]

Nicaragua was in a state of chaos and uncertainty: the politicians and businessmen, both foreign and domestic, were profiting, and the Nicaraguan people were suffering the consequences. The United States was imposing its might over their resources, and Nicaragua was reduced to a "Banana Republic:" a politically unstable country whose economy is largely dependent on exporting limited-resource products.[9] After several decades of internal political struggle, injustice at the hands of corrupt officials, and bending to the will of outside forces, the Nicaraguan people had finally had enough. In 1927, under the leadership of Augusto Calderón Sandino, the Liberal Revolution of Nicaragua had begun.

The purpose of this research paper is to study Augusto Calderón Sandino's status as a revolutionary, during Nicaragua's periods of occupation. This will be done by analyzing Sandino as a man and a revolutionary—what motivated him, what his goals were, and how he achieved his goals—to determine which of the primary types of revolutions; liberal, political, nationalist, military, professional, or agitator—Sandino was, and what influence, impact, and legacy he has had in Nicaragua and neighboring Central American countries.

This will be done through a variety of methods, including the use of academic and journalistic sources, such as Bernard Nalty's "Marine Corps Historical Reference Pamphlet: The United States Marines in Nicaragua" and Harry Vanden's "Democracy and Socialism in

---

[5] Langley, Lester D. *The Banana Wars: United States Intervention in the Caribbean, 1898–1934*. Kentucky: University Press of Kentucky, 1983.

[6] Bailey, Thomas, A. "Interest in a Nicaragua Canal, 1903-1931." *The Hispanic American Historical Review*. Vol. 16, No. 1 (Feb., 1936), pg. 2-28.

[7] Langley, Lester D. *The Banana Wars: United States Intervention in the Caribbean, 1898–1934*. Kentucky: University Press of Kentucky, 1983.

[8] "Bryan-Chamorro Treaty." 14 August, 1914. Treaties and Other International Agreements. The United States and Nicaragua.

[9] White, Richard Alan. *The Morass: United States Intervention in Central America*. New York: Harper & Row, 1984.

Sandinista Nicaragua." Sources contributing to this study will include secondary sources from both the United States and Latin America. An array of primary sources will also be used to supplement the research. In terms of primary sources, contemporary articles from Time Magazine, words by Calvin Coolidge, and letter written by Sandino, as well as his manifesto, will also be analyzed. There were a few other outstanding sources that were intended to be used, unfortunately, some of these sources, while valuable, did not have sufficient information to draw from, or information fell outside the purview of my inquiries. All sources previously mentioned, and many more, will be used to answer the questions regarding Augusto Sandino as a revolutionary and his impact on Latin America.

Contextual Essay

During the early years of the 20th century, socio-political revolutions were igniting around the world, this was particularly true in Central America—a region that had seen instability in the previous several decades. The United States saw itself as the defender of these tumultuous Latin American nations, and, under the declarations in the Monroe Doctrine, sought to occupy them to maintain order and suppress anarchy and chaos. Later, the same Monroe Doctrine would also be used to protect American business interests in the region, and keep United States-friendly Latin American leaders in power.

The Monroe Doctrine was a principle of the United States' foreign policy, regarding dominion of North and South American nations, introduced in 1823.[10] Although the term "Monroe Doctrine" itself was not coined until about1850, President James Monroe first stated the doctrine during his seventh annual State of the Union Address to Congress. In it, Monroe stated that further efforts by European nations to colonize land in the Americas, or to interfere with their politics, would be viewed as acts of aggression, and that the United States would intervene on their behalf.[11] While declaring their intention to defend free American nations, the doctrine noted that the United States would neither interfere with existing European colonies nor Europe itself. At the time when the Monroe Doctrine was issued, nearly all Latin American colonies of Spain and Portugal had achieved, or were on the verge of achieving, independence.[12]

By the end of the 19th century, the Monroe Doctrine was considered a defining moment in American foreign policy, and one of its defining tenets. Many United States politicians, and several United States presidents, including Ulysses S. Grant, Theodore Roosevelt, John F. Kennedy, Ronald Reagan have invoked it.[13]

Excepts from the doctrine itself state:

---

[10] Murphy, Gretchen. *Hemispheric Imaginings: The Monroe Doctrine and Narratives of U.S. Empire*. North Carolina: Duke University Press, 2005.

[11] "Monroe Doctrine." December, 1823. State of the Union Address. The United States.

[12] Graham, Richard. *Independence in Latin America: A Comparative Approach* (2nd edition). United States: McGraw-Hill, 1994.

[13] Murphy, Gretchen. *Hemispheric Imaginings: The Monroe Doctrine and Narratives of U.S. Empire*. North Carolina: Duke University Press, 2005.

"The occasion has been judged proper for asserting, as a principle in which the rights and interests of the United States are involved, that the American continents, by the free and independent condition which they have assumed and maintain, are henceforth not to be considered as subjects for future colonization by any European powers.—We owe it, therefore, to candor and to the amicable relations existing between the United States and those powers to declare that we should consider any attempt on their part to extend their system to any portion of this hemisphere as dangerous to our peace and safety. With the existing colonies or dependencies of any European power we have not interfered and shall not interfere. But with the Governments who have declared their independence and maintained it, and whose independence we have, on great consideration and on just principles, acknowledged, we could not view any interposition for the purpose of oppressing them, or controlling in any other manner their destiny, by any European power in any other light than as the manifestation of an unfriendly disposition toward the United States."[14]

The terms and impact of the Monroe Doctrine remained relatively consistent, with only minor variations, for more than a century. Its objective to guard the freedom of the newly independent nation of Latin America from European intervention, and avoid situations which could make the New World a metaphoric pie to be carved up by the Old World powers, was upheld. In later decades, it became more so that the United States could exert its own influence in the region undisturbed, but its original intentions may have been true enough. The doctrine asserted that the New World and the Old World were to remain distinctly separate spheres of influence, regardless of the reasons why. After 1898, with America's victory over Spain in the Spanish-American War, Latin American lawyers and intellectuals re-interpreted the Monroe Doctrine to be more about multilateralism and non-interventionism. Under President Franklin Roosevelt, in 1933, the United States went along with the new interpretations.[15]

---

[14] "Monroe Doctrine." December, 1823. State of the Union Address. The United States.

[15] Scarfi, Juan Pablo, "In the Name of the Americas: The Pan-American Redefinition of the Monroe Doctrine and the Emerging Language of American International Law in the Western Hemisphere, 1898-1933." *Diplomatic History*. Vol. 40 No. 2 (2014) United States pg. 189-218.

When you think of the United States in modern times, you think of it as a world power—the last remaining, and currently only real Superpower. Whether or not this changes in the near future is up for debate, but for the moment, and as has been the case for the last 100 years, the United States is a top power in the world. At the time of the Monroe Doctrine's inception, it was really a case of "his bark is worse than his bite." In the early-mid 19<sup>th</sup> century, the United States was a new nation. It was confident because it had just won its independence from one of the top powers in Europe, but it was by no means anywhere near a world power. It was a regional power at best. The United States government feared the emerging European powers that spawned from the Congress of Vienna around 1815: France had already agreed to restore the Spanish Monarchy in exchange for Cuba,[16] with the end of the revolutionary Napoleonic Wars, Prussia, Austria, and Russia formed the Holy Alliance to defend monarchism and restore Bourbon rule to Spain and its colonies.[17] The United States felt threatened, and it had to act big to prevent any potential or hypothetical invasions and re-conquests. This is, in part, where the Monroe Doctrine came from. The United States had to let Europe think that it could defend itself and its newly emerging, neighboring, nations.

Despite the proclamation, the United States could likely do nothing if the forces of Europe truly wished to re-conquer them and their neighbors. They had played a bluff and hoped that Europe would not call it. In a surprising turn of events, however, it was not the United States who first defended and invoked the Monroe Doctrine, but rather Britain.[18]

Great Britain shared the general objective of the Monroe Doctrine. Although their position was different, Britain wanted to declare a joint statement to keep other European powers from further colonizing the New World—with Spain and Portugal on the cusp of losing their colonies, and France already seeing the majority of theirs taken from them, Britain could remain the sole colonial power in the Americas and further their potential as the top power in Europe. British Foreign Secretary George Canning wanted to keep the other European powers out of the New World, for fear that its trade with the New World would be harmed if the other European

---

[16] Cressen, William Penn. *The Holy alliance: the European background of the Monroe Doctrine*. United Kingdom: Oxford University Press, 1922.

[17] Cressen, William Penn. *The Holy alliance: the European background of the Monroe Doctrine*. United Kingdom: Oxford University Press, 1922.

[18] Lawson, Leonard Axel. *The Relation of British Policy to the Declaration of the Monroe Doctrine*. United Kingdom: Columbia University, 1922.

powers colonized it further. For many years after the Monroe Doctrine was declared, Britain, through the Royal Navy, was the nation actually enforcing it, for the United States lacked sufficient naval capabilities at the time. The United States of America resisted a joint statement because of the recent War of 1812, with Britain; leading to the Monroe administration's unilateral statement. Despite this, both nations invoked and enforced the doctrine.[19]

Despite the United States taking up the position as an isolationist nation at the time, the idea of the Monroe Doctrine was already in the minds of the American government during George Washington's presidency. Alexander Hamilton expressed his desire for the United States to control the sphere of influence in the western hemisphere, particularly in North America, despite dying some decades before the Monroe Doctrine's inception. Hamilton already wanted to establish the United States as a world power, as mentioned in the Federalist Papers.[20] This desire may have stemmed from the fact that the European countries controlled far more of the continents than the United States of America itself did.

Due the United States' apparent lack of any military power, particularly naval power, the doctrine was largely disregarded internationally. That is, of course, until the British Royal Navy enforced it as part of the Pax Britannica. Reactions in Latin America were initially generally favorable, but with some suspicious. According to author, John Crow:

"Simón Bolívar himself, still in the midst of his last campaign against the Spaniards, Santander in Colombia, Rivadavia in Argentina, Victoria in Mexico—leaders of the emancipation movement everywhere—received Monroe's words with sincerest gratitude."[21]

The leaders and revolutionaries of Latin America, at the time, knew that the United States wielded very little power, especially before the British expressed their support of it. They appreciated the gesture, but figured it was unenforceable and unrealistic to even consider. These

---

[19] Lawson, Leonard Axel. *The Relation of British Policy to the Declaration of the Monroe Doctrine*. United Kingdom: Columbia University, 1922.

[20] Hamilton, Alexander, James Madison, & John Jay. *The Federalist Papers*. United States: Courier Corporation, 2014.

[21] Crow, John A. "Areil and Caliban". *The Epic of Latin America* (4th ed.). Berkeley: University of California Press, 1992.

sentiments soon changed and gradually grew to concern. With the United States' intervention in the Spanish colony of Cuba in 1898, and Theodore Roosevelt's Roosevelt Corollary being added to the Monroe Doctrine in 1904 (which proclaimed the right of the United States to intervene in Latin America in cases of "flagrant and chronic wrongdoing by a Latin American Nation"),[22] the leaders of Latin America knew that they had to be wary, or fall victim to Roosevelt's "Big Stick" ideology. Some leaders, seeking to retain and extend their leadership roles beyond traditional terms, sought to use the Monroe Doctrine in alliance with the United States. One Chilean minister, Diego Portales, wrote in a letter: "—but we have to be very careful: for the Americans of the north [the United States], the only Americans are themselves."[23] The United States' emergence as "hemispheric policemen" had begun, and it was apparent that the Monroe Doctrine would devolve to protect only their interests.


Thesis

Augusto Calderón Sandino was a Nicaraguan revolutionary who combated the United States Marines and the Nicaraguan federal government in the late 1920s and early 1930s. This essay will explore Augusto Calderón Sandino's credibility as a revolutionary as well as establishing what category, or categories, of revolutionary that Sandino falls under. In doing so, it will be analyzing his role as a liberal revolutionary, political revolutionary, nationalist revolutionary, military revolutionary, professional revolutionary, and an agitator. There will also be an analysis of his ideologies and beliefs, how he served the masses, his methods for sparking revolution, his experience and leadership skills, and his revolutionary career in general to establish his validity as a Latin American revolutionary. It will also determine his goals and methods of revolution, establish what the lasting effect of his campaign was, and determine which category of revolutionary that Sandino most falls into place with.

Of the many different categories of revolutionary that Sandino could fall under, the strongest arguments could be for him being either a liberal revolutionary, political revolutionary,

---

[22] Roosevelt Corollary. 1904. State of the Union Address. The United States.

[23] Uribe, Armando, *El Libro Negro de la Intervención Norteamericana en Chile*. México: Siglo XXI Editores, 1974.

9

nationalist revolutionary, military revolutionary, professional revolutionary, or an agitator, but before one can file him under one or several of these categories, it is important to understand how each differs from one another, and what makes them unique.

A liberal revolutionary is a political revolutionary who exhibits the liberal beliefs of his region and seeks to change the government of his country or region to accommodate those beliefs. Liberal revolutionaries primarily wanted free trade, land redistribution among the masses, and secularized education. They supported progressivism but despised neo-colonialism and were more centralist in their political ideologies.[24] The primary focus for liberals at this time was combating foreign imperialism and neo-colonialism. Liberal revolutionaries are also more focused on rallying the common folk—the lower, oppressed, classes. In the case of Sandino, these would have been the mestizos and indigenous peoples of Nicaragua. In Augusto Calderón Sandino's Manifesto, issued on July 1, 1927,[25] Sandino starts his declaration by addressing the "Nicaraguans—the Central Americans—and the Indo-Hispanic Race,"[26] already strengthening his foundation as a liberal revolutionary. Further in the manifest, Sandino continues to affirm that he has liberal ideologies and wishes to depose the conservative oligarchs who were then wielding power in Managua. He wrote:

> "—my idealism is based upon a broad horizon of internationalism, which represents the right to be free and to establish justice—. The oligarchs, or rather, the swamp geese, will say that I am a plebeian—. My greatest honor is that I come from the lap of the oppressed, the soul and spirit of our race, those who have lived ignored and forgotten, at the mercy of the shameless hired assassins who have committed the crime of high treason, forgetful of the pain and misery of the Liberal cause that they pitilessly persecuted—."[27]

---

[24] Sandino, Augusto César. "Sandino Manifesto." *latinamericanstudies.org*. 1 July, 1927. Web. 8 Feb, 2012. http://www.latinamericanstudies.org/sandino/sandino7-1-27.htm

[25] Sandino, Augusto César. "Sandino Manifesto." *latinamericanstudies.org*. 1 July, 1927. Web. 8 Feb, 2012. http://www.latinamericanstudies.org/sandino/sandino7-1-27.htm

[26] Sandino, Augusto César. "Sandino Manifesto." *latinamericanstudies.org*. 1 July, 1927. Web. 8 Feb, 2012. http://www.latinamericanstudies.org/sandino/sandino7-1-27.htm

[27] Sandino, Augusto César. "Sandino Manifesto." *latinamericanstudies.org*. 1 July, 1927. Web. 8 Feb, 2012. http://www.latinamericanstudies.org/sandino/sandino7-1-27.htm

In this section of the manifesto, Sandino actually states that the conservative oligarchs are persecuting the liberal cause, Sandino's cause. Further evidence in the manifesto includes statements where Sandino questions the nationality and loyalty of the "mercenaries who still demand the right to rule over us as oligarchs, supported by the invader's [American's] Springfield-[rifle]s." [28] This statement provides some insight into how the Nicaraguan government was operating at the time; supporting American imperialism and neo-colonialism. It also confirms Sandino's desire to rid Nicaragua of the American-backed government.

The final piece of evidence to support Augusto Calderón Sandino's classification as a liberal revolutionary, also comes from his manifesto. In the ninth paragraph, Sandino exclaims:

"For myself and for my companions in arms who have not betrayed the Liberal revolution, who have not faltered and who have not sold our weapons to satisfy our own ambition, the revolution continues, and today more than ever before it is powerful because only those who have displayed the valor and self-denial that every Liberal should possess remain involved in it." [29]

These excerpts provide strong grounds to classify Sandino as a self-admitted liberal Revolutionary, but that does not necessarily mean that he would not better fit into a different classification.

A political revolutionary is a revolutionary who seeks to change the current status and mode of operations of the current government, whether this change is for a liberal government or a conservative government. A liberal revolutionary could be listed as a sub-category for a political revolutionary. By already establishing Augusto Calderón Sandino's validity as a liberal revolutionary, it is safe to say that he automatically qualifies as a political revolutionary. But could Sandino truly be considered a political revolutionary if he had no apparent interest in placing himself at the head of Nicaragua's government?

Nationalist revolutionaries are revolutionaries who seek to unite a group of people that share common traits and values, such as ethnicity, heritage, culture, religion, language, or life

[28] Sandino, Augusto César. "Sandino Manifesto." *latinamericanstudies.org*. 1 July, 1927. Web. 8 Feb, 2012. http://www.latinamericanstudies.org/sandino/sandino7-1-27.htm
[29] Sandino, Augusto César. "Sandino Manifesto." *latinamericanstudies.org*. 1 July, 1927. Web. 8 Feb, 2012. http://www.latinamericanstudies.org/sandino/sandino7-1-27.htm

values, as the embodiment of a nation. Their goal is to either establish a homeland for this united entity, or put into power a government that is for the people, will accommodate the people, and is run by the people. Using excerpts from Sandino's Manifesto, a valid argument can also be made to classify Sandino as a nationalist revolutionary.

As mentioned previously, Sandino starts his manifesto by addressing the Nicaraguan people, Latin Americans, and Indo-Hispanic people, setting a common ground and addressing a distinct group of people who make up the embodiment of the nation of Nicaragua. In the third paragraph he states; "I am a Nicaraguan and I am proud because in my veins flows above all the blood of the Indian race, which by some atavism encompasses the mystery of being patriotic, loyal, and sincere."[30] By writing this he places himself among the common people, strengthening nationalist ties among the lower classes. Just after this, at the beginning of the fourth paragraph, Sandino exclaims that "the bond of nationality gives me the right to assume responsibility for my acts," which also strengthens his ties to the people and his categorization as a nationalist revolutionary.[31]

After briefly establishing his nationalist identity and his ties to the common people, he attacks the nationalism, or lack-there-of, of the current government while questioning their loyalties to the Nicaraguan people at the same time. Sandino declares:

"Sixteen years ago Adolfo Díaz and Emiliano Chamorro ceased to be Nicaraguans. Ambition killed their right to their nationality because they ripped from its staff our country's flag, the symbol that envelops all Nicaraguans. Today that flag flies limply and in shame because of the ingratitude and indifference of its sons, who do not made a superhuman effort to free it at once from the claws of the enormous eagle with its curved beak bloody with the blood of Nicaraguans. Meanwhile in the Campo de Marte military base that flag that murders weak nations now waves, the enemy of our race and of our language."[32]

---

[30] Sandino, Augusto César. "Sandino Manifesto." *latinamericanstudies.org*. 1 July, 1927. Web. 8 Feb, 2012. http://www.latinamericanstudies.org/sandino/sandino7-1-27.htm
[31] Sandino, Augusto César. "Sandino Manifesto." *latinamericanstudies.org*. 1 July, 1927. Web. 8 Feb, 2012. http://www.latinamericanstudies.org/sandino/sandino7-1-27.htm
[32] Sandino, Augusto César. "Sandino Manifesto." *latinamericanstudies.org*. 1 July, 1927. Web. 8 Feb, 2012. http://www.latinamericanstudies.org/sandino/sandino7-1-27.htm

This accusation that Sandino makes about the Nicaraguan government having a non-nationalist agenda and lack of devotion to the Nicaraguan people, reaffirms his own portrayal as a nationalist revolutionary. If having a lack of nationalism is a flaw, which Augusto Sandino makes an extensive effort to criticize in his opposition, then by default he would naturally be a nationalist himself.

A Military revolutionary is a person who seeks to changes in a government by changing or utilizing military tactics and warfare to rise to power and overthrow a government. As with the other categories of revolutionary which Augusto Calderón Sandino could be described as, there is a strong argument that can be used to classify him as a military revolutionary.

Although Sandino does not outright call himself a military revolutionary or call his revolution a military revolution, in his manifesto, there are militaristic aspects briefly mentioned and described in it. Sandino swears by his sword that he will defend the national honor and redeem the oppressed from his government and the "invaders of the Fatherland."[33] Sandino does at one point call his followers soldiers, stating in the paragraph; "I am firmly convinced that when they have killed the last of my soldiers, more than a battalion of their own men will have died in my wild mountains"[34] and that he hopes to convince other members of the Indo-Hispanic race that in "the mountains of the Andean Cordillera there exists a group of patriots who will know how to die like men, in open battle, in defense of their national honor."[35] This statement, along with further reinforcing his role as a nationalist revolutionary while at the same time implicating his role as a military revolutionary. Sandino also address the Americans, whom he refers to as "morphine addicts" with a phrase stating; "I await you before my patriotic soldiers."[36] Other suggestions in Sandino's Manifesto about his role as a military revolutionary, and how he sees himself, can be seen in other excepts like:

---

[33] Sandino, Augusto César. "Sandino Manifesto." *latinamericanstudies.org*. 1 July, 1927. Web. 8 Feb, 2012. http://www.latinamericanstudies.org/sandino/sandino7-1-27.htm

[34] Sandino, Augusto César. "Sandino Manifesto." latinamericanstudies.org. 1 July, 1927. Web. 8 Feb, 2012. http://www.latinamericanstudies.org/sandino/sandino7-1-27.htm

[35] Sandino, Augusto César. "Sandino Manifesto." latinamericanstudies.org. 1 July, 1927. Web. 8 Feb, 2012. http://www.latinamericanstudies.org/sandino/sandino7-1-27.htm

[36] Sandino, Augusto César. "Sandino Manifesto." latinamericanstudies.org. 1 July, 1927. Web. 8 Feb, 2012. http://www.latinamericanstudies.org/sandino/sandino7-1-27.htm

"I wish to assure the governments of Central America, especially that of Honduras, that my attitude should not cause them concern. They should not think that, because my forces possess more than enough strength to invade their territory, I would do so with the intention of overthrowing them. No. I am not a mercenary, but rather a patriot who does not allow outrageous assaults upon our sovereignty."[37]

This paragraph further pushes for Sandino to be classified as a military revolutionary, while at the same time he denies his role as a military leader, claiming one as a patriot instead. However, just because he denies being a military revolutionary, does not mean that he is not one.

Another section that indicates Sandino as a military leader as well as a nationalist states:

"the magnificent slogan symbolized by our *red and black* flag—should not be a victim violated by the Yankee adventurers who were invited here by the four horrid individuals who still claim to have been born in this land."[38] This is the final paragraph which in Sandino's Manifesto, making a total of four, that implies any indication that Sandino is a military revolutionary. Most other paragraphs have more nationalist than military implications, such as the paragraph where Sandino proclaims;

"The world would be an unbalanced place if it allowed the United States of America to rule alone over our canal, because this would mean placing us at the mercy of the Colossus of the North, forcing us into a dependent and tributary role to persons of bad faith who would be our masters without justifying such pretensions in any way."[39]

His seems to want to bring an end to threats and occupation by the United Sates rather than lead a military and a country.

As far as being a professional revolutionary is concerned, tt would be a small challenge to claim that any revolutionary is not a professional revolutionary, since a professional revolutionary is someone who dedicates their there life and their work to their revolutionary

---

[37] Sandino, Augusto César. "Sandino Manifesto." latinamericanstudies.org. 1 July, 1927. Web. 8 Feb, 2012. http://www.latinamericanstudies.org/sandino/sandino7-1-27.htm
[38] Sandino, Augusto César. "Sandino Manifesto." latinamericanstudies.org. 1 July, 1927. Web. 8 Feb, 2012. http://www.latinamericanstudies.org/sandino/sandino7-1-27.htm
[39] Sandino, Augusto César. "Sandino Manifesto." latinamericanstudies.org. 1 July, 1927. Web. 8 Feb, 2012. http://www.latinamericanstudies.org/sandino/sandino7-1-27.htm

cause, claiming their cause as their occupation. Apart from temporarily holding a job as a clerk in a Nicaraguan mine, Sandino has not really had any other known occupation. Although his father was a wealthy landowner, Augusto Calderón Sandino was born out of wedlock, leaving him to be raised primarily by his mother in poor, working class, conditions. Unable to follow in his father's footsteps and not wanting to live a hard life of manual labor and degradation, he was captivated by an uprising against the corrupt Nicaraguan government, which was put down by the United States military. After attempting to kill a prominent townsman who made degrading remarks toward his mother, Sandino fled to Mexico, where he found temporary work at an oil refinery and witnessed the Mexican revolution first-hand.[40] Upon returning to Nicaragua in 1927 with a liberal, revolutionary-inspired, agenda, he left any form of a gainful employment and set out to bring the common people of Nicaragua out of misery and bring an end to the elitist government which was supported by the imperialistic foreigners—the Americans. Thus, Augusto Calderón Sandino dedicated his life to his revolutionary cause, permitting him to be classified as a "professional revolutionary."[41] This same year he composed his manifesto.[42]

The final classification of a revolutionary that Sandino falls under is that of an Agitator. An agitator is a person who gets the common people exited for change, is enthusiastic as a speaker, and addresses the people directly, prompting them, the peasants, to be the instigators of change. With the opening statement of his manifesto being addressed "To the Nicaraguans, to the Central Americans, to the Indo-Hispanic Race"[43] and the closing statement being;

"Fellow citizens: Having expressed my ardent desire to defend my country, I welcome you to my ranks without regard to your political tendencies, with the one condition that you come with good intentions to defend our nation's honor. Because keep in mind that you can fool all of the people some of the time, but not all of the people all of the time."[44]

---

[40] Aurelio Navarro-Génie, Marco. "Augusto "César" Sandino: messiah of light and truth." New York; Syracuse University Press, 2002. Print.

[41] Aurelio Navarro-Génie, Marco. "Augusto "César" Sandino: messiah of light and truth." New York; Syracuse University Press, 2002. Print.

[42] Sandino, Augusto César. "Sandino Manifesto." latinamericanstudies.org. 1 July, 1927. Web. 8 Feb, 2012. http://www.latinamericanstudies.org/sandino/sandino7-1-27.htm

[43] Sandino, Augusto César. "Sandino Manifesto." latinamericanstudies.org. 1 July, 1927. Web. 8 Feb, 2012. http://www.latinamericanstudies.org/sandino/sandino7-1-27.htm

[44] Sandino, Augusto César. "Sandino Manifesto." latinamericanstudies.org. 1 July, 1927. Web. 8 Feb, 2012. http://www.latinamericanstudies.org/sandino/sandino7-1-27.htm

It is very evident that Sandino was initially an agitator, addressing his manifesto to the people, rather than addressing it toward the government or the United States or Nicaragua. Sandino also displays a sense of humbleness in his address, trying not to sound like a man who is power hungry or specifying himself as superior to every other peasant by addressing his manifesto as being written from "San Albino Mine, Nueva Segovia, Nicaragua, Central America,"[45] the place which he was working at the time before dedicating his efforts to revolution.[46]

Now that it has been established that Augusto Calderón Sandino is in fact a revolutionary, it is important to firmly establish which classification of revolutionary that he most embodies, as well as confirming his ideologies, analyze how he served masses, his methods of making revolution, what his experience were, what kind of leader he was, and how his revolutionary career relates to a larger history of Latin America and what his lasting significance was.

Out of all of the different types of revolutionaries that Sandino could be classified as, the strongest could be made that Sandino was a liberal revolutionary. This classification also automatically classifies Sandino as a political revolutionary, but since he had no apparent desire to goal to become the new President of Nicaragua, a lone classification of "political revolutionary" might be overlooked.

In many ways he is a liberal-nationalist. Although part of his revolutionary campaign was to drive foreign imperial powers, such as the United States, out of Nicaragua, Sandino's primary focus was to overthrow the elite, conservative, government and bring liberal reforms to the country. Being influenced and inspired by the Mexican revolution in the early twentieth-century,[47] Sandino was fighting for the rights of the common, poor, people in the country. When Sandino applied for the job as a mine clerk when he returned from Mexico, he did so not because he needed the money, but because it kept him close to Nicaragua's working class, and provided the perfect opportunity to spark a revolutionary fire.[48] Sandino preached to the miners about fare wages, the right to form unions, the need for safe working conditions, and the realization that

---

[45] Sandino, Augusto César. "Sandino Manifesto." latinamericanstudies.org. 1 July, 1927. Web. 8 Feb, 2012.
[46] Aurelio Navarro-Génie, Marco. "Augusto "César" Sandino: messiah of light and truth." New York; Syracuse University Press, 2002. Print.
[47] Aurelio Navarro-Génie, Marco. "Augusto "César" Sandino: messiah of light and truth." New York; Syracuse University Press, 2002. Print.
[48] Aurelio Navarro-Génie, Marco. "Augusto "César" Sandino: messiah of light and truth." New York; Syracuse University Press, 2002. Print.

none of this was possible while the Nicaraguan government was selling out its own people in favor of good standings with the United States. Thus Sandino set in motion the Sandino Rebellion, further military intervention from the United States, who had been occupying Nicaragua since 1910 during the Banana Wars, and the eventual implementation of a Liberal Government in Nicaragua.[49] While possible, few revolutions get off the ground without military or armed conflict.

Even those that do can often end in such a war. Sandino was a military leader, his revolution waged war against his own government and that of the United States—so would the classification of "military revolutionary" fit Sandino? It could, but as previously mentioned, Sandino was not interested in installing himself as president, he was not interested in taking power for himself, and that may be where he falls outside of the classification. Countless military revolutionaries of the past have overthrown their governments and installed themselves in office—whether they intend it to be temporary so that they might guide their new government and country to a better future, or whether they intend to remain "president for life." This does not seem to be Sandino's intentions.

As far as being a professional revolutionary is concerned, Sandino does indeed appear to qualify as one (as do most revolutionaries). Sandino dropped his desires for gainful employment in order to focus his life on the revolution. He did maintain a job as a mine clerk for a while, but this was to further his agenda, not because he needed money. So while he is in fact a professional revolutionary, a different classification might be more appropriate, such as that of a liberal or liberal-nationalist revolutionary.

While starting his career out as somewhat of an agitator, after Sandino picked up support, giving speeches and motivating the populace seemed to be less of an objective. He still made statements and wrote letters, but he had already motivated the masses, he had no further need to preach. The later part of Sandino's career was more action-oriented rather than speech-oriented, for this reason, it would seem that "agitator" would not be the bet suited title of Sandino.

---

[49] Nalty, Bernard C. "Marine Corps Historical Reference Pamphlet: The United States Marines in Nicaragua." Washington D.C.; United States Marine Corps, 1968. Print.

Although he led his own rebellion and is recognized as the key leader of the rebels in Nicaragua, there had been vain attempts by other revolutionaries for several years to remove the Nicaraguan government. When the United States Marines briefly pulled out of Nicaragua in 1925, several small revolutions, being headed by various rebel groups, broke out across the country.[50] In 1926, after failing to quell the rebellions with his own military and police force, the officially recognized president of Nicaragua, Adolfo Diaz, sent out a plea to the United States for military aide. [51] This opened up the door for Augusto Calderón Sandino to make a name for himself by doing what was morally correct by fighting the colossus of the north and trying to bring ownership back to the people, whereas the United States military was doing what it saw as being legally correct by coming to the aide of the recognized Nicaraguan president and trying to restore the country to the relatively peacefully time when the United States had previously occupied the country.[52]

Through letter addressing the United States military leaders, the people of Nicaragua, and the Nicaraguan government, Sandino made clear the reforms that he wanted and voiced the concerns of the working class Nicaraguans who were too fearful to voice their own opinions. In a letter addressed to political candidates in 1928, Sandino makes it clear that he and the working class were not satisfied with the new government of Nicaragua. The letter reads;

"Themes in Respect to the Candidates—That the [Nicaraguan] populace would not let itself be fooled again by [José María] Moncada. That Nicaragua has been capacitated to direct the destinies of the nation without the necessity of confiding in Moncada, who has several times proved himself to be a traitor. That we will back no caudillo who proclaims himself, because then we would be in danger of dictatorship, and we permit ourselves to invite the public to meditate well in electing their candidates, and that they choose men

---

[50] Coolidge, Calvin. "Intervention in Nicaragua." mtholyoke.edu. Record, 69th Congress, 2 Sess., pp. 1324-1326, 1926. Web. 8 Feb, 2012.
[51] Nalty, Bernard C. "Marine Corps Historical Reference Pamphlet: The United States Marines in Nicaragua." Washington D.C.; United States Marine Corps, 1968. Print.
[52] Coolidge, Calvin. "Intervention in Nicaragua." mtholyoke.edu. Record, 69th Congress, 2 Sess., pp. 1324-1326, 1926. Web. 8 Feb, 2012.

who can defend with loyalty the principles of our credo and the interests of the country in general. That they can fix their looks on patriotic personalities—."[53]

Moncada, who had been an ally with Sandino in helping overthrow Diaz and fighting against the United States Marines, had been chosen as the new president of Nicaragua, taking office in 1929. Moncada upon accepting the presidency had tried to persuade Sandino that the United States military would leave the country once it was more politically stable. This did not sit well with Sandino. Despite bringing a liberal government into power in Nicaragua, Sandino was not convinced that the new government was completely liberal, or entirely representative of the people, as Moncada had been appointed rather than elected by the Nicaraguan people.

Moncada also appeared to have loyalties to the United States, branding him in Sandino's mind as a traitor and not the legitimate leader of the people of Nicaragua. This belief caused Sandino to continue in a solo revolution, gaining him further fame and helping him carve out his place in history.[54]

From other letters addressed to and from Sandino, we can analyze some characteristics of his as well as his leadership skills and his persistence to rid Nicaragua of oligarchic rule and foreign imperialism. In a letter addressed to commanders of the United States Marines, written on January first of 1928, addressed from the "Fort of the Defenders of the Sovereignty of Nicaragua,"[55] Sandino makes his goals and determination to succeed clear.

"Dear Sirs, I have the honor of answering your communication dated the 27th of last December. I cannot accept the conference that you propose in your letter. I wonder because you offer me guarantees when I am an outlaw, furthermore, it is up to us to give guarantees since we are the genuine sons of Nicaragua. We shall comply with what we have said before: that we will not retire because as long as the punitive Yankees are in our territory, we shall always hold to arms. In the moment that I am answering your letter

[53] Sandino, Augusto César. "Circular." sandinorebellion.com. January 1928. Web. 8 Feb, 2012. http://www.sandinorebellion.com/EDSNDocs/1928a/edsn280101c.html
[54] "José María Moncada." *Biografías y Vidas*. Biografiasyvidas.com. 2012. Web. Mar, 20, 2012.
[55] Sandino, Augusto César. "Letter to John Nevin Sayre & Robert C. Jones." *sandinorebellion.com*. 1 January 1928. Web. 8 Feb, 2012. http://www.sandinorebellion.com/EDSNDocs/1928a/edsn280101DSandino.html

we are looking at the burning of the town of Quilalí done by the pirate Yankees. Oh! Damned flesh that shall have its reward!!"[56]

From this letter we can see that Sandino was not impressed or satisfied with the results of the Liberal Revolution that implemented what he saw as a faux liberal government. Sandino did not wish to negotiate with the Americans or the government, what Sandino wanted was the implementation of a true liberal government that would bring democracy to Nicaragua and rights to the working class. Sandino was not willing to compromise or settle with half of his demands, rights and security for the working class, a real liberal government in power, the American leaving Nicaragua, being met, he was determined to reach all of his goals or die trying.

Part of reason that the United States was so interested in maintaining an active military presence in Latin America early in the twentieth century was a reemergence of a "new manifest destiny" and the desire to maintain hemispheric dominance. The United States also saw Nicaragua as a strategic position to build a canal that would link the Atlantic and Pacific Oceans. After the Panama Canal was built in Panama, Nicaragua remained strategically important for maintaining a defense of the new inter-ocean passage way.[57] Another reason why the united states was interested in maintaining a military presence in Latin America was to "create professional, nonpartisan, political militaries in these nations" that could be potential allies and would not fall to socialist of communist ideologies.[58] Whether it was because of military, political, or economic interests, the United States' primary reason for reoccupying Nicaragua after a several month exit was to "ensure the adequate protection of all American interests in Nicaragua, whether they be endangered by internal strife or by outside interference in the affairs of that republic," as stated by President Calvin Coolidge.[59] The Americans were concerned about their properties and business' and originally demanded that Nicaraguan president Diaz protect the American interests. Diaz, lacking the man power to fight the rebels and keep peace, requested

---

[56] Sandino, Augusto César. "Letter to John Nevin Sayre & Robert C. Jones." *sandinorebellion.com*. 1 January 1928. Web. 8 Feb, 2012. http://www.sandinorebellion.com/EDSNDocs/1928a/edsn280101DSandino.html

[57] LeoGrande, William M. "The Revolution in Nicaragua: Another Cuba?" *Foreign Affairs Vol. 58, No. 1.* New York; Council on Foreign Relations, Fall, 1979. Print.

[58] Polk, Freddy L. "Building Armies for Democracy: U.S. Attempts to Reform the Armed Forces of Cuba (1906-1909) and Nicaragua (1927-1933)." Fort Leavenworth, KS; Army Command and General Staff College, 05 JUN 1987. Print.

[59] Coolidge, Calvin. "Intervention in Nicaragua." mtholyoke.edu. Record, 69th Congress, 2 Sess., pp. 1324-1326, 1926. Web. 8 Feb, 2012.

that the United States instead send the Marines as a peace-keeping and anti-rebel force.[60] The Marines stayed in Nicaragua as long as they felt it was necessary to ensure American interests. They may have indented to stay longer, but with the onset of the Great Depression and Augusto C. Sandino's Nicaraguan guerrilla troops fighting back against them, it became too costly for the United States government to maintain their deployment. The Marines were ordered to withdraw in 1933.[61]

Augusto Calderón Sandino's influence and the lasting effect of his revolution can be seen all over Latin America in different ways. The immediate result of Sandino's revolution was the implementation of a real liberal government in Managua, under the leadership of newly elected president Juan Bautista Sacasa in January 1933, that was for the rights of the working-class people, and the exodus of the United States Marines from Nicaragua as part of Franklin Delano Roosevelt's "Good Neighbor Policy." In his inaugural address on March 4th, 1933, Roosevelt stated;

"In the field of world policy I would dedicate this nation to the policy of Good Neighbor—the neighbor who resolutely respects himself and, because he does so, respects the rights of others; the neighbor who respects his obligation and respects the sanctity of his agreement in and with a world of neighbors. We now realize as we have never realized before our interdependence on each other; that we cannot merely take, but also must give as well."[62]

Everything seemed to be going well in the small Latin American nation: Sandino had won his revolution, the United States Military was leaving Nicaragua, a democratically elected president presided over the capital, and Sandino vowed to never attack an American civilian visiting Nicaragua again.[63] This prosperity was short lived however. Not three years after Franklin Roosevelt dedicated the United States to the good neighbor policy and opened up a relationship

---

[60] Nalty, Bernard C. "Marine Corps Historical Reference Pamphlet: The United States Marines in Nicaragua."Washington D.C.; United States Marine Corps, 1968. Print
[61] "The United States Marines in Nicaragua." United States: Historical Branch, G-3 Division Headquarters, U.S. Marine Corps, 1961.
[62] Crawley, Andrew. "Somoza and Roosevelt: Good Neighbour Diplomacy in Nicaragua, 1933-1945." New York; Oxford University Press, 2007. Print.
[63] Unknown Author, "NICARAGUA: Sandino Presents Arms." *Time Magazine*, Monday, Feb. 13, 1933. Print.

with Juan Sacasa's government, Anastasio Somoza deposed the young democratic government and established a reign of terror that would last for decades, until his assassination.[64]

The lasting effects of Sandino's revolution, however, lie within the overthrow of Sacasa's government by Somoza and Somoza's assassination of Sandino on February 21, 1934 while he was return from a round of peace talks with Somoza.[65] There was a large belief among the Nicaraguan people that Franklin Roosevelt was connected with Juan Somoza when he overthrew the government and had Sandino assassinated, causing a large distrust of Americans in Nicaragua for decades. This had a particularly strong effects on foreign policy when Sandino's rebel group, the Sandinista National Liberation Front (FSLN), became a successful political party in 1979 and had their presidential candidate, Daniel Ortega, took office in Nicaragua in 1985.[66] This caused trained foreign relation between the United States and Nicaragua that persist today. With the FSLN taking power the country, they fought to undo the Nicaragua's drastic underdevelopment, deal with the impoverished populations and mismanaged resources, as well as turn around the countries poor health and education systems and improve poor working conditions for the lower class that had been implemented during the countries time under conservative dictatorship.[67]

On a larger scale, other Latin American countries were inspired by Sandino and his revolution. Between 1890 and 1933, United States Presidents have used the United States military in Latin America without congressional approval.[68] It was inspirational for the other Latin American countries to witness a small rebellion in Nicaragua grow into a revolution that could successfully expel the American armed forces from their soil. Sandinismo would take off and spread among the Spanish speaking nations of America. In the 1980s the Sandinista

[64] Crawley, Andrew. "Somoza and Roosevelt: Good Neighbour Diplomacy in Nicaragua, 1933-1945." New York; Oxford University Press, 2007. Print.
[65] Unknown Author, "NICARAGUA: Murder at the Crossroads." *Time Magazine*, Monday, Mar. 05, 1934. Print.
[66] Crawley, Andrew. "Somoza and Roosevelt: Good Neighbour Diplomacy in Nicaragua, 1933-1945." New York; Oxford University Press, 2007. Print.
[67] Babb, Florence E. "After the Revolution: Neoliberal Policy and Gender in Nicaragua." *Latin American Perspectives Vol. 23, No. 1*. California; Sage Publications, Winter, 1996. Print.
[68] Crawley, Andrew. "Somoza and Roosevelt: Good Neighbour Diplomacy in Nicaragua, 1933-1945." New York; Oxford University Press, 2007. Print.

government introduced and adjustment and stabilization programs in Nicaragua. Similar neoliberal programs spread throughout other parts of Latin America soon after.[69]

Before the rise of Sandinismo in Nicaragua and around Latin America, Latin Americans could not comprehend or change their present realities because they had lost their sense of history and revolution past. Many other liberal revolutionaries had lost sight of what they were fighting for. The beginning of a modern national consciousness in Nicaragua and the rest of Latin America began with Sandino's revolution. Although the Liberal Reform Movement was not born in Nicaragua, but rather in Mexico, the Liberal movement that Sandino sparked in his own country had a wider effect on the other Latin American countries who viewed Mexico as another Colossus to the North, like the United States, and were inspired by the success of the small nation's revolution and fight against the United States.[70]

In conclusion, it has been established that Augusto Calderón Sandino is a Latin American revolutionary, specifically a liberal or liberal-nationalist revolutionary. This is in part because of his specific mentioning of "liberal revolution" in his manifesto, and his dedication to bringing back rights, power, and better standards of living for the working class citizens of Nicaragua. He was also dedicated to overthrowing a government that he did not consider to be truly Nicaraguan and wanted to establish a true Liberal Government that was more concerned with the well-being of the people, than pleasing the United States Government. The temporary result of Sandino's revolution was the establishment of a true liberal government in Nicaragua, before it was overthrown by another dictator's regime.

It can also be said that Sandino's liberal revolution was responsible for the modern liberal Reform seen in other Latin American countries. Sandino's revolutionary group later transformed into a political party, the FSLN, which would later take power in a free and fair election in 1985, helping spur the neo-liberal movement in Latin America. The modern Liberal Reform Movement in Latin America can be attributed to the efforts of Augusto Calderón Sandino and his revolutionary army in the Nicaraguan Revolution between 1927 and 1933.

---

[69] Babb, Florence E. "After the Revolution: Neoliberal Policy and Gender in Nicaragua." *Latin American Perspectives Vol. 23, No. 1*. California; Sage Publications, Winter, 1996. Print.
[70] Vanden, Harry E. "Democracy and Socialism in Sandinista Nicaragua." United Kingdom; Lynne Rienner Publishing, 1993. Print.

Secondary Sources

Aurelio Navarro-Génie, Marco. "Augusto "César" Sandino: messiah of light and truth." New
   York; Syracuse University Press, 2002. Print.

Babb, Florence E. "After the Revolution: Neoliberal Policy and Gender in Nicaragua."
   Latin American Perspectives Vol. 23, No. 1. California; Sage Publications,
   Winter, 1996. Print.

Bailey, Thomas, A. "Interest in a Nicaragua Canal, 1903-1931." *The Hispanic American
   Historical Review*. Vol. 16, No. 1 (Feb., 1936), pg. 2-28.

Crawley, Andrew. "Somoza and Roosevelt: Good Neighbour Diplomacy in Nicaragua, 1933-
   1945." New York; Oxford University Press, 2007. Print.

Cressen, William Penn. *The Holy alliance: the European background of the Monroe Doctrine*.
   United Kingdom: Oxford University Press, 1922.

Crow, John A. "Areil and Caliban". *The Epic of Latin America* (4th ed.). Berkeley: University of
   California Press, 1992.

Graham, Richard. *Independence in Latin America: A Comparative Approach* (2nd edition).
   United States: McGraw-Hill, 1994.

"José María Moncada." *Biografías y Vidas*. Biografiasyvidas.com. 2012. Web. Mar, 20, 2012.

Langley, Lester D. *The Banana Wars: United States Intervention in the Caribbean, 1898–
   1934*. Kentucky: University Press of Kentucky, 1983.

Lau Gutiérrez, William. *Proceso de la intervención norteamericana en Nicaragua (1909 –
   1913)*. Encuentro: Revista Académica de la Universidad Centroamericana, 1989.

Lawson, Leonard Axel. *The Relation of British Policy to the Declaration of the Monroe
   Doctrine*. United Kingdom: Columbia University, 1922.

LeoGrande, William M. "The Revolution in Nicaragua: Another Cuba?" *Foreign Affairs
   Vol. 58, No. 1*. New York; Council on Foreign Relations, Fall, 1979. Print.

Murphy, Gretchen. *Hemispheric Imaginings: The Monroe Doctrine and Narratives of U.S. Empire*. North Carolina: Duke University Press, 2005.

Nalty, Bernard C. "Marine Corps Historical Reference Pamphlet: The United States Marines in Nicaragua." Washington D.C.; United States Marine Corps, 1968. Print.

Polk, Freddy L. "Building Armies for Democracy: U.S. Attempts to Reform the Armed Forces of Cuba (1906-1909) and Nicaragua (1927-1933)." Fort Leavenworth, KS; Army Command and General Staff College, 05 JUN 1987. Print.

Scarfi, Juan Pablo, "In the Name of the Americas: The Pan-American Redefinition of the Monroe Doctrine and the Emerging Language of American International Law in the Western Hemisphere, 1898-1933." *Diplomatic History*. Vol. 40 No. 2 (2014) United States pg. 189-218.

"The United States Marines in Nicaragua." United States: Historical Branch, G-3 Division Headquarters, U.S. Marine Corps, 1961.

Uribe, Armando, *El Libro Negro de la Intervención Norteamericana en Chile*. México: Siglo XXI Editores, 1974.

Vanden, Harry E. "Democracy and Socialism in Sandinista Nicaragua." United Kingdom; Lynne Rienner Publishing, 1993. Print.

White, Richard Alan. *The Morass: United States Intervention in Central America*. New York: Harper & Row, 1984.

Wünderich, Volker. *Sandino: Una biografía política,* Nicaragua: Editorial Nueva Nicaragua,1995.

Primary Sources

"Bryan-Chamorro Treaty." 14 August, 1914. Treaties and Other International Agreements. The United States and Nicaragua.

Coolidge, Calvin. "Intervention in Nicaragua." mtholyoke.edu. Record, 69th Congress, 2
    Sess., pp. 1324-1326, 1926. Web. 8 Feb, 2012.

Hamilton, Alexander, James Madison, & John Jay. *The Federalist Papers*. United States:
    Courier Corporation, 2014.

"Monroe Doctrine." December, 1823. State of the Union Address. The United States.

Roosevelt Corollary. 1904. State of the Union Address. The United States.

Sandino, Augusto César. "Circular." sandinorebellion.com. January 1928. Web. 8 Feb,
    2012. http://www.sandinorebellion.com/EDSNDocs/1928a/edsn280101c.html

Sandino, Augusto César. "Letter to John Nevin Sayre & Robert C. Jones."
    *sandinorebellion.com.*    1    January    1928.    Web.    8    Feb,    2012.
    http://www.sandinorebellion.com/EDSNDocs/1928a/edsn280101DSandino.html

Sandino, Augusto César. "Sandino Manifesto." *latinamericanstudies.org.* 1 July, 1927. Web. 8
    Feb, 2012. http://www.latinamericanstudies.org/sandino/sandino7-1-27.htm

Unknown Author, "NICARAGUA: Sandino Presents Arms." United States: *Time Magazine*,
    Monday, Feb. 13, 1933. Print.

Unknown Author, "NICARAGUA: Murder at the Crossroads." United States: *Time Magazine*,
    Monday, Mar. 05, 1934. Print.

# YOUR KNOWLEDGE HAS VALUE

- We will publish your bachelor's and master's thesis, essays and papers

- Your own eBook and book - sold worldwide in all relevant shops

- Earn money with each sale

Upload your text at www.GRIN.com
and publish for free